Big and Little
in the Bible

written by Tina Brewer

illustrated by John Ham

Library of Congress Catalog Card No. 85-62948
© 1986. The STANDARD PUBLISHING Company, Cincinnati, Ohio
Division of STANDEX INTERNATIONAL Corporation. Printed in U.S.A.

God told Noah to build a BIG boat, because He was going to fill the whole world with water. The boat would keep Noah safe. Noah obeyed God and built the BIG boat.

Jesus taught from a LITTLE boat. People liked to listen to Jesus. Jesus told the people that God loved them.

Saul was a BIG king. He was taller than all the other men. God wanted him to be king.

Josiah was a LITTLE king. He was only eight years old when he became king. Josiah was a good, LITTLE king.

God let a BIG fish swallow Jonah. He did this because Jonah had tried to run away. But God took care of Jonah inside the BIG fish.

After three days the BIG fish spit Jonah out on dry land. Jonah did not run away from God again.

A small boy had two LITTLE fish and five loaves of bread for his lunch. The boy gave his LITTLE fish and loaves to Jesus. Jesus fed many people with the fish and loaves. The boy was glad to share his lunch.

Goliath was a BIG man. Everyone but David was afraid of Goliath, because he was so BIG. God helped David kill Goliath.

Zaccheus was a LITTLE man. He wanted to see Jesus. Zaccheus climbed up in a tree so he could see Jesus.

Jesus saw Zaccheus and asked if He could eat lunch with him. Zaccheus was glad to eat lunch with Jesus.

God put a BIG star in the sky. This BIG star showed the wise men where baby Jesus was. They followed the BIG star for many nights. The wise men worshiped Jesus when they found Him.

The stars in the sky look LITTLE because
they are so far away. God put them in the sky
with the moon to shine at night.

A BIG offering was taken to repair the temple. The people filled up a BIG chest with money each day. There was enough money to make the temple look beautiful again.

A poor widow gave a LITTLE offering at church. God was happy with her LITTLE offering because she gave all she had.

God loves BIG men and women. Jesus
told many people that He loved them.

God loves LITTLE boys and girls. Jesus liked to hold and talk to little children.

BIG men and women can help God by giving money to church,

by praying to God,

and by loving other people.

LITTLE boys and girls can help God by giving their money to church,

by praying to God,

and by being friends with other children.

The Bible shows us how God uses both BIG and LITTLE. So it doesn't matter if you are BIG or LITTLE. You can help God, too.